OREGON TRAIL

Volume 1

Oregon Country Series

[signature: Rick Steber]

Rick Steber

Illustrations by Don Gray

NOTE

The *OREGON TRAIL* is the first book in an Oregon Country Series. Each volume contains stories written by Rick Steber which first appeared in his syndicated newspaper column, "Oregon Country".

Oregon Trail
Volume 1
Oregon Country Series

Bonanza Publications, Ltd.
Box 204
Prineville, Oregon 97754

INTRODUCTION

One of the great things about Oregon is that our history lies so close to the surface. It was our grandparents and parents who were the pioneers. Even today people are alive who made the wagon crossing over the Oregon Trail.

The first wagon train arrived in Oregon in 1843. It is estimated one-half million emigrants traveled the great trail west, until the era ended in the early 1900s with the advent of the automobile.

Stretches of the Oregon Trail are still visible as ruts; ruts carved into the earth, worn by time and masked by wildflowers, sagebrush and trees. The trail remains as a testimonial to the special breed of individuals who endured the 2,000 miles of unforgiving country and the constant threat of Indian attack to forge a new life in Oregon. They existed day to day on a dream that life would be better in Oregon. Sweeping into the Willamette Valley they staked claims in the wilderness, built homes, cultivated the virgin soil. This flood of emigrants assured that one day the Oregon Country would become part of the United States.

THE PRAIRIE SCHOONER

Some ordered their prairie schooners brand new from the factory, while others simply had the local blacksmith make the necessary adjustments on the farm wagon.

The Conestoga wagon, which originated in Pennsylvania in the mid-1700s, was the familiar prairie schooner with ends higher than the sides to keep the contents from spilling out going up or down steep hillsides.

The Conestoga had one disadvantage, though; it was big and heavy and for that reason many emigrant guide books recommended the Yankee wagon. The Yankee was much lighter and stronger. It was made of well-seasoned, close-grained oak that grew in the hills of New Hampshire and could be purchased for around $200.

Families heading west spent many days readying their wagons, filling them with everything they could possibly need for a five-month journey. When packing was completed, a canvas cover was stretched over the top. If they followed the advice of experienced guides, the coverings were always doubled to provide greater protection against the weather. Many emigrants added their own personal touch by painting slogans or their destinations on the canvas.

A wagon was worthless unless it had good wheels and Joel Palmer, who led many wagon trains westward, could not emphasize their importance strongly enough. "Wagon wheels," he suggested, "should be at least one and three-quarters inches wide; three-inches would be best of all for crossing the oftentimes loose, sandy roads. The rims should be, at the minimum, three-quarters of an inch thick and fastened to the felloes with bolts rather than nails. Hub boxes should be at least four inches thick."

If the prairie schooner were well-seasoned and well-made and their oxen faithful and strong, the pioneers had a fighting chance to arrive in Oregon with a wagon that could be used for chores and transportation on their new farm.

WAGONS WEST

Pioneers fought their way across 2,000 miles of Indian country, bouncing over rocks, choking on dust and fording swollen rivers. Families, crowded into canvas-covered wagons, struggled to start a new life, to carve a home in the wilderness of the Pacific Northwest.

The first year of the great migration, 1843, three hundred wagons carried nine hundred men, women and children over the Oregon Trail. Two years later three thousand people gathered at the flood gates in St. Joseph, Missouri, anxious to begin their overland journey into the unknown. Joel Palmer, leader of the wagon train, informed them, "The loading should consist of provisions and apparel, a necessary supply of cooking fixtures, a few tools .... everything in the outfit should be as light as the required strength will permit, no useless trumpery should be taken."

The pioneers had to plan for more than a five-month, cross-country journey. Everything that was necessary to build a new home and to begin farming had to be packed. Palmer suggested the minimum food essentials for each person consist of two hundred pounds of flour, seventy-five pounds of bacon, ten pounds of rice, five pounds of coffee, twenty-five pounds of sugar, ten pounds of salt, two bushels of dried beans and dried fruit, one bushel of corn and corn meal and one keg of vinegar.

Good shoes and warm clothes were a must for every person. Each man was required to carry at least one rifle and plenty of ammunition. Oxen were considered the best animals to pull the heavy wagons; they were strong and dependable and Indians were not likely to steal them.

Palmer broke the wagons into groups of twenty-five and by the middle of April, with men driving the stubborn green teams, women and babies crowded into the back of the wagons, older children walking and driving the loose stock, the caravan started west.

OXEN AND BUFFALO

The early pioneers discovered a curious fact about oxen while crossing the broad sweep of the Plains. Oxen go absolutely crazy when smelling buffalo.

One pioneer related, "It is an odd thing that when oxen smell the fresh trail of the buffalo they paw and bellow as if they smelt fresh blood. If you have ever tried to stop a runaway oxen team, you know what hard work it is."

An 1845 wagon train, captained by Presley Welch, had the misfortune of a runaway. At first the driver tried to thwart the headlong charge by hauling back on the reins but the oxen kept running. Riders came alongside and tried to turn them, first one way and then the other, but they plowed ahead over the uneven ground.

The wagon bounced along behind in sharp jolts like the popping of a whip. In this mad dash two oxen ran themselves to death and were drug by the others. When they could no longer breathe they, too, stopped. The men cut the throats of the dead animals and butchered them. The pioneers found the meat "tough and stringy".

Later in the journey the guide came riding at a dead gallop, shouting to swing the wagons into a circle and corral the oxen inside. He said a big band of buffalo was stampeding and would be there within minutes.

The herd passed dangerously close to the circle of wagons and the oxen were frantic, trying repeatedly to join the stampeding buffalo, but none were able. The pioneers were forced to stay in camp several hours until the guide deemed the buffalo trail was cool enough that the oxen would be manageable.

WAGON TRAIN JUSTICE

John Smith was a disagreeable old cuss and as the wagons of the Missouri company pulled out of St. Joe that spring morning in 1852, he cursed the others because they raised dust.

Along the way to Oregon a young boy was orphaned and the last person on earth who should have taken him in was old man Smith; but that was what happened. From the very beginning he despised the boy, complaining he was depleting his stock of rations among other things. The boy could do nothing right. The oxen received too little or too much feed. The cook fire was either too hot or not hot enough.

For his part the boy tried; his efforts were belittled and cursed. Others in the wagon train came to the boy's defense. They advised Smith to change his ways. Smith rebuffed them, said he would do whatever he pleased.

As miles rolled on the division between the man and the boy became more pronounced. One day the boy was walking alongside the wagon. A wheel fell off and Smith flew into a rage, accusing the boy of causing it. At night camp Smith was overheard muttering, "I'll fix him."

In the morning Smith seemed to have reversed his mood and cheerily asked the boy if he would like to go rabbit hunting. The man and the boy walked away from the wagon train. The boy never returned.

The old man stood trial for murder and was found guilty. Since there were no trees, three wagons were pushed together and the tongues lifted to form a triangle. A rope was fastened to the top of the tongues, a noose fashioned and wagon train justice ran its swift course.

A HARD TRAIL

There was a father, mother and nine children in the Smith family. They started west over the Oregon Trail in 1846; not all of them would make it to the Willamette Valley.

William Smith was captain of a number of wagons trying to blaze a new route through southern Oregon. He led his family and the others into Canyon Creek in the Umpqua range but a sudden wind trapped them in downed trees.

"We will have to give up the wagons and ride the oxen," the others told William, but he was of fighting stock.

"I've got a wife and nine children," he told them. "Louisa is deathly sick and you know Thaddeus is crippled and cannot ride. I am taking my spring wagon. We can make it. But do as you please, if you have no confidence in me. Maybe I'm the only man among us with any guts...."

As William was exhorting his men he suddenly sank to his knees, cried, "Lord, have mercy upon me!" and died of a heart attack.

The spring wagon that he was determined to take to the end of the trail was torn apart and used to make a coffin. His wife Ellen cried over his grave and then packed herself and the nine children on the two oxen.

The rough trip took its toll and little Louisa's condition deteriorated and she died. The last words Louisa whispered to her mother were, "Bury me deep, pile rocks on top. I don't want the wolves to get me."

Somehow Ellen was able to make it safely to the Williamette Valley with the remainder of her family intact. Starting with a donation land claim she carved out an existence and raised her eight children.

THE NAME

Mrs. Masiker had heard all the good reasons for coming to Oregon but she was not convinced. Her father had started west the year before with plans to locate a homestead and send for his family. But he had vanished and no one had seen nor heard from him since he departed.

During that year of her father's absence, she had married George Masiker. Shortly after the wedding he informed her they were moving to Oregon. She was torn between going west and trying to find out what had become of her father, and staying with her mother. In the end she was a dutiful wife and went with her husband.

They joined a wagon train bound for Oregon. They traveled for several weeks and then one evening, after supper was cooked and the dishes washed, Mrs. Masiker took a walk. She went down by the Platte River, sat on a rock and watched the cranes fly over. The light wind shimmered the reflection of the sun on the top of the water.

She tried to imagine what Oregon must look like and remembered the things she had been told and what she had read. The daydream ended as the sun began to tumble from the sky.

Mrs. Masiker started back for camp. On the way she noticed the shoulder blade of a buffalo stuck in the ground. Did it mark a grave? She could see writing on the bleached bone. She bent to read the faded lead markings. There was a name — Solomon Trumble — her father.

THE PINE BOX

Grandma Gaylor was crying as she bent and gave little Leonora a goodby kiss. The wagon started forward, the girl gave her grandmother one last kiss and hurried to catch up with her folks and the other members of the Illinois wagon train. They were off to Oregon.

That afternoon they came to a long hill and the women and children stepped down from the wagons to save the oxen from having to pull their weight. Leonora was taking a nap in the wagon, awoke with a start to find her father still driving, but her mother and her sisters no longer in the wagon.

Leonora pulled back the canvas cover, saw the others walking off to the side of the wagon away from the billowing dust. Leonora swung over the sideboard, balanced for a second and then fell. The rear wheel passed over her. She cried out in pain as her small thigh bone snapped under the weight of the wagon.

The wagon train's doctor set the broken leg and ordered a narrow pine box be built. He gave the measurements so the injured leg would fit in it very tightly.

Leonora traveled with her leg in the pine box all the way to Oregon. Sixty-four years later, in 1917, Leonora was honored by the Oregon Pioneer Association. They made note that Leonora had come west in a pine box and lived to tell about it.

MERCY ARROW

Around the fire that night members of the wagon train attempted to dissuade a traveling companion from going out on his own. This was Blackfoot country, a dangerous land. Stories of Blackfoot deprivations were told but the man, a Missourian, had his mind set. He insisted on making a short trapping foray and promised he would overtake the wagon train by the time it hit Oregon.

In the morning the wagons continued west while the lone Missourian drifted north setting beaver traps in likely spots. After several successful days, and after having come across neither Indians nor Indian sign, the man felt safe.

One afternoon he was knee deep in water retrieving a drowned beaver, rifle out of reach on the bank, when he had the strange sensation he was being watched. He looked and on both sides of the creek were Indians, mounted and wearing war paint. He made a lunge for his rifle but one of the braves simply slid off his horse and grabbed it. The Missourian was marched to the Indian camp.

That night, as the fire leaped into the blackness, the Indians danced and held council. The Missourian, concerned about his fate, asked the Indian standing guard what was happening. He was told, "Talk about you die."

The Missourian was resigned to the fact he was going to soon meet his Maker but wanted to know how it was to be accomplished. The guard answered, "You burn."

"Kill me now!" pleaded the prisoner but the guard did nothing as the others gathered a great quantity of firewood and heaped it around a lone tree. The Missourian was led forward, his arms tied behind him around the tree, and coals were brought over to start a fire at his feet. Again he cried out, "Kill me!"

Flames were licking at him. The heat was unbearable. An arrow whistled through the air, struck him in the heart. The fire consumed a dead man.

BAD APPLE

The bad apple always rots first and so it was among a group of men traveling west in a wagon train. In this instance the bad apple was a renegade from Missouri.

The party regarded him with suspicion from the moment he signed on and the farther they traveled west, the more reason they had to watch him. The renegade continually complained and found fault, particularly with the friendly manner in which members of the wagon train treated the Indians. The renegade claimed the only way to treat an Indian was to shoot first and ask if he were friendly later.

The wagon train passed an Indian village on the bank of the Platte River and the emigrants were able to enlist the services of an Indian to guide them. The bad apple tried to pick a fight with the guide and that evening after dark, a single rifle shot resounded. At the edge of the camp the body of the Indian was discovered. The renegade was gone.

Members of the wagon train discussed their predicament. Some were for burying the Indian and going their way; others felt if they buried the Indian his tribe would come looking, discover the grave and assume they had committed the deed.

At last it was decided one among them would return the body to the Indian village and explain the circumstances. To be fair, straws were drawn. Next morning the wagon train continued west. The unlucky drawer rode east with the body of the dead Indian scout lashed to the back of his saddle.

He approached the Indian village late in the afternoon and was escorted to the chief's tepee. The chief listened to the explanation, accepted the body and made signs the white man was free to leave. He did so. Behind him, keeping a distance, rode a delegation of Indians.

They did not try to overtake him, but when they arrived at the death camp they broke away from the Oregon Trail and began searching. Before long there were several shots fired. The braves had found the bad apple.

DEATH ON THE TRAIL

During the year 1852 fatal cholera wiped out ten percent of the emigrants. Seven persons in one family were buried in a single grave. And a scout reported that following the Oregon Trail from the Platte River to Fort Laramie, a distance of 400 miles, he counted twelve graves to the mile.

Death rode with the Abbott family in 1852. Their wagon made it as far as the Platte River before the father died of dreaded cholera. He left behind a wife and five children.

"We laid him to rest where the Old Emigrant road left the fork of the Little Blue River and passed on," wrote John Abbott, one of the sons.

"The cholera claimed able-bodied men, women and children by the score. Panic prevailed. You could see men and women on their bended knees asking God to show mercy on their loved ones.

"Our only fatality passing through the cholera belt was Father. As a whole the train lost 30 percent.

"We reached the Snake River, which was a region where mountain fever was prevalent, and Mother took ill. She died and we buried her on the banks of the Powder River. From then on us five kids were on our own. When things like that happen it makes you grow up in a hurry.

"We made it, reached the Willamette Valley, and ever after this was home — the promised land."

LONG TIME IN COMING

Before they got to the Oregon Trail the William McCown family had trouble.

The Mississippi river steamer on which they took passage hit a floating snag and began to take on water. The captain turned toward shore and in the excitement steered for Illinois though the wagon emigrants wanted to land on the Missouri side. An old riverboat captain, on board as a passenger, took the wheel and made a beeline for Missouri. The steamer ran aground. Every man, woman and child escaped but their possessions, their teams and wagons, were lost.

The young McCown family was destitute and the bad times forced William to take a job following his blacksmith trade. He was able to purchase a two-wheel cart and they traveled west, William doing blacksmith work where he found it. They were in Henry County, then Post Oak and on to Kansas. William's wife died there.

By the time they reached the Cascades it was late in the year. They were trapped for a time by a blizzard but fought their way through.

The McCowns reached the Willamette Valley and located a place to winter in the hills near Oregon City. That year there was two feet of snow on the level. Only one animal, the saddle horse, survived the winter. The next spring he became a plow horse.

SLAVE WOMAN

As an Oregon-bound wagon train was being organized a few families and friends decided they could make better time on their own without the inconvenience of being part of a large group of wagons. They moved a few miles ahead of the main body.

Three days out of St. Joseph, Missouri, the group made camp, ate supper and went to bed, not taking the precaution of setting a guard. So far they had not encountered any Indians.

Around midnight Indians sneaked into camp and surprised the sleeping pioneers. Only two members of the party were spared, a woman and her twelve-year-old son. The others were killed.

The woman was placed on an Indian pony and her son set behind her. As the pony was led from the terrifying scene of burning wagons the woman looked back and saw her husband move his hand. She whispered to her son, told him his father was still alive and that when she tapped him on the leg he was to drop off and hide. When it was safe he was to run back to main wagon train for help.

The Indians, excited at the successful raid, did not notice the boy slide off into tall weeds. He ran with fear pushing him until he came to the scene of the attack. The wagons were only embers but his father was not where he had been left. The son overtook his father, who was crawling on hands and knees, and ran on into the main camp.

The woman remained captive for a number of years. She suffered and endured a great deal, but because of the unceasing efforts of her husband and son she eventually was rescued by a group of trappers who purchased her from the Indians.

BRAVE SQUAW

They were in Indian country. Miralda Greenstreet was edgy and kept checking around her for signs of trouble. She was two miles behind the small Oregon-bound wagon train, driving the loose stock.

Without warning fifty braves boiled over the ridge nearest Miralda. Their faces were painted with war paint. It would be useless to run. Miralda slipped from her saddle, stood beside her horse clutching the reins.

The Indians came close, peering at her with piercing black eyes. Miralda met their gaze, masking her terror behind a calm exterior. Her reins were jerked away. The Indians spun their ponies in unison and raced toward a spot a hundred yards away. They arranged themselves in pairs and with a string of sharp yips and blood-curdling whoops they came straight at Miralda. As they passed, on either side, they swung tomahawks at her head. The cold metal flashed so close it whistled the air and made her skin crawl.

Pass after pass the war party continued the game, waiting for Miralda's own fear to cause her to flinch. She stood like carved stone.

At last the braves tired of their macabre fun. They came in and circled tightly around her.

"Brave squaw," one of them told her. Then they rode away, leaving Miralda absolutely alone on the broad sweep of the plains.

PEGLEG

He had lost a leg during the Civil War; and though his name was Simpson, everyone called him Pegleg.

Pegleg came over the Oregon Trail in 1866. He was the brunt of jokes because in addition to his obvious handicap, he also stuttered and was painfully shy. The children mimicked him.

When word got around about Pegleg's unnatural fear of Indians, it only made matters worse. There were a few demented souls who would sneak up on him and give forth a war whoop, just to watch his reaction.

Then came the afternoon, within sight of Fort Laramie, that Pegleg's wagon became mired in mud while crossing a marshy area. The other wagons went on. When they were a mile away, someone noticed and they had a laugh at Pegleg's expense before a small group started back to give him a hand.

They were halfway there when Indians suddenly appeared and began circling Pegleg's wagon. Shots were fired. And then they saw him — Pegleg — standing on the bed of his wagon with the canvas cover tossed back, turning this way and that, shooting Indians.

The Indians pulled back. Before the men from the wagon train could reach Pegleg he succeeded in prying his wooden leg from the knothole where it was stuck. He never confessed he had simply made the best of a bad situation. Instead, he basked in their warm accolades commending his courage.

DOWN TO LONGJOHNS

At camp in the Grande Ronde Valley, Andrew Masters sat away from the others. He was a troubled man. His wife was expecting their first born any day. If they stayed with the wagon train it would be at least a week before they could cross the mountains and reach Doctor Whitman's mission.

Andrew came to the realization he and his wife would have to go alone. The next morning, at first light, they departed on saddle horses and the others in the wagon train waved, called encouragement.

The trail led into the mountains. Late in the afternoon, in the middle of a thunderstorm, Andrew lost the trail and could not relocate it. But he knew they needed to travel north.

When at last they started down, Mrs. Masters felt sudden, sharp pains and once in a while would groan involuntarily. They came to a spring and Andrew stripped off his shirt, wet it and gave it to his wife. She held it to her forehead and wiped the back of her neck.

For two days they wandered without food or water. The morning of the third they awoke to discover the horses missing. Mrs. Masters cried she did not want to give birth if the baby was doomed. Shortly after saying that, two Indians rode into camp. They claimed to know where the horses were and offered to trade.

"We don't have anything to trade," Andrew informed them. One of the Indians suggested a deal could be struck if Andrew were willing to put up his shirt, trousers and the red bandanna he wore around his neck.

Within an hour the Indians returned with the horses. Andrew went down to longjohns and then he and his wife rode toward where the Indians had motioned they would find the Whitman Mission.

They reached the mission and Mrs. Masters immediately went under Doctor Whitman's care. The next morning she gave birth to a strong, healthy baby.

FIREWORKS

Monroe Stayles, his wife and their daughter Inez, came west over the Oregon Trail. They crossed the Cascades on the Barlow toll road and arrived at Oregon City thinking the excitement of the journey was over.

A level spot near the Willamette River was chosen as a camping spot and the Stayles family went about evening chores. It did not bother Monroe when a few Indians, who were camped nearby, paid a visit. He figured Indians living so close to civilization must be friendly. But then he saw how much attention one of the Indians, the chief, was paying to Inez.

Inez was only twelve years old but her appearance belied her age. She had raven-black hair, dark eyes and was very pretty. The chief fell in love with her.

Indian tradition dictated a man trade for his bride. The chief approached Monroe, told him of his intentions and offered robes, horses and furs in exchange for the girl. Monroe ran him out of camp.

It was nearly dark when Mrs. Stayles went to the nearby spring for a pail of water. She did not return and Monroe was about to look for her when an Indian messenger came into camp with the message Mrs. Stayles was being held captive and would be released only after Inez was given to the chief.

Thinking quickly, Monroe told the messenger, "Tell your chief if my wife is not returned immediately the Great Spirit will make fire come down like rain on your village."

The Indian departed. Monroe retrieved a small box of fireworks that he had brought all the way from Oklahoma. He walked toward the Indian village and when he was still a hundred yards out, he lit the first rocket. It went high above the tepees and exploded. Before another rocket could be launched Mrs. Stayles was set free.

19

BOILED BUFFALO HIDE

A small group of friends came west together. They endured the long wagon trip and at The Dalles took passage on a ferry for the remainder of the journey.

Coming through Cascades Rapids a strong wind hit their raft from the side and capsized them. They were thrown in the icy water and forced to fight for their lives.

By some miracle all landed safely on a narrow strip of shoreline that butted up against a solid basalt wall hundreds of feet high. They counted their blessings that all were alive, then got down to the bare facts of survival.

One had flint and was able to start a driftwood fire. There was no food to eat the first evening but the next day a boiling pot and a buffalo hide washed ashore. Since the hide was the only thing remotely associated with food they scraped off the hair, cut the hide into strips, and placed them in the pot to boil.

At Fort Vancouver, friends were awaiting their arrival. When the raft did not come they became worried and arranged for an Indian to search the river. He located the lost group on their solitary spit of beach and returned to the fort for help. The little group was finally rescued after having spent seven days and nights on the isolated beach, subsisting only on the boiled buffalo hide.

MASSACRE ROCKS

Twenty-five Iowa families made up the small wagon train that reached Fort Hall the first of August, 1862. That night the fiddle was brought out and a dance was held as the pioneers celebrated having come 1,200 miles.

But 800 miles of difficult travel lay in front of them before they would reach the promised land, the Willamette Valley.

The wagon train followed along on the south side of the Snake River for several days before, late one afternoon, the lead driver spotted Palisade, a prominent landmark, and called out. Word was passed back from one wagon to the next.

Palisade was an unusual formation of rocks that obstructed the course of the Oregon Trail. The wagons were forced to detour through the rocks in single file.

The little train had reached the narrowest spot when there came war whoops, rifle shots and a volley of arrows. A war party of Indians were hiding among the rocks. The pioneers could not circle their wagons. They could not even turn around. They whipped the oxen and tried to charge through.

Nine emigrants were killed in the ambush. Ever after, Palisade was known as Massacre Rocks.

THE PRICE WAS DEATH

The Winters family was coming west and having a tough time of it. Dreaded cholera struck their wagon train. Hiram Winters watched for symptoms in his wife Rebecca and the children but sickness passed them by until one evening near Scotts Bluff, Nebraska.

As they made camp Rebecca said she was not feeling well. She complained of stomach pain and dizziness, and before dinner was cooked she lay down on the bed in the wagon.

The swiftness of the disease took the family by surprise. One minute Rebecca was resting comfortably and the next she was gasping for air. Just before midnight William went to take her a cup of broth and discovered she was no longer among them.

William mourned the parting the only way he could, he kept his hands busy. He took a spare wagon rim, picked up a hammer and chisel and in the fire light began etching a grave marker.

William finished his work as the sun came over the horizon. Etched on the rounded rim were the words, "Rebecca Winters, age 50 years". Rebecca was buried and the rim was used to mark the grave. For many years the rim endured as a shrine to the memory of a wife and mother.

THE CANNON
AND THE MULE MOLLY

Not a day passed that members of the small wagon train did not fear Indian attack. But across the Plains and even over the Rocky Mountains the Indians they encountered were friendly. And then they hit the Oregon Country.

On a sagebrush flat, cut by deep dry washes that could hide men on horseback, came a blood-curdling war whoop and the pounding of horses' hooves. Indians, faces painted, rode the length of the wagon train firing arrows.

The captain called for the wagons to be circled and drivers quickly obeyed, but the attackers persisted. They rode in close, shooting arrows. The pioneers took pot shots at them with black powder rifles.

The pioneers had been planning for a moment like this. Before leaving Missouri they had purchased a small cannon and a mule named Molly to carry it. When the Indians poised for another attack, Molly was led to the front. Without taking time to unpack her, the cannon was loaded and Molly turned so that her hindquarters as well as the opening of the cannon were pointed toward the group of Indians.

A belch of white smoke. Molly was knocked forward. A split second later the roar of the cannon reached the Indians. They grunted in surprise and a few moments later the chief, his right arm held in a sign of peace, came riding slowly toward the pioneers.

He spoke solemnly, saying the Indians could not compete with the white man who could "shootum mule."

TRAIL OF FEATHERS

Members of an 1854 wagon train to Oregon had several encounters with hostile Indians. One of those times occurred when they arrived at a settlement of several cabins scattered around a series of springs.

They stopped and called, but could not raise a soul. That seemed strange and several of the men investigated, found the cabins ransacked and the inhabitants missing.

"Let's look around outside," suggested one of the men. They fanned out in the sagebrush looking for tracks or other sign but found nothing. It appeared the inhabitants of the small settlement had disappeared into thin air.

The searchers were about to give up when a feather was discovered. There was another feather, another, and another. Evidently a leaky mattress had been part of the plunder.

A guard was left with the wagons to protect the women and children while another group saddled horses. They proceeded slowly, following the trail of feathers through foothills until at last coming to a high ridge. Several of the men dismounted and crawled to a position where they could peer over the edge without being skylined. In the valley below they saw Indians dancing around a fire, their captives were tied and lying face down in the dirt.

The pioneers pulled back and an attack plan was quickly scratched in sand; they would surround the camp and swoop in from all directions at once. It worked perfectly. The settlers, to the last man, were rescued.

BUFFALO WALL

Buffalo stampedes struck fear into the hearts of the early-day pioneers. A fellow by the name of Crabtree gave a personal account of living through a buffalo stampede.

He told how a line of dust stretching from horizon to horizon was the first detectable sign of a buffalo stampede. How, from so many hooves striking the earth, there was the rolling of thunder ever louder, ever closer. All they could do was circle the wagons and take actions to try to split the herd.

Crabtree claimed, "I had the fastest horse in camp, breed horse, high strung and fast. I led the charge, firing guns in the air; but to no avail. And when the herd threatened to overrun me I turned around and ran with it. To me it seemed like trying to outrun a flood.

"My horse went down. He probably hit a gopher hole. I got knocked off, was dazed there for a second, looked up and saw the buffalo were almost on me. I managed to crawl over against my horse. A couple of buffalo went around me, one leaped over the top and the next one hung up. After that it was like dominoes. The bodies piled up, around and over me. I didn't move. I was safe enough were I was.

"The herd swept past, the thunder was going away and the choking dust was beginning to settle when I was able to squirm my way from beneath the mass of dead and dying.

"I fully expected the wagon train to have been obliterated by the buffalo. But to my complete amazement it was safe, spared because my buffalo wall had split the herd."

26

SAVED BY A DOUGHNUT

Upon crossing the Snake River into Oregon the 36 members of the Ohio train felt like celebrating. Wagons were circled and women began cooking a special dinner while the men stood around in groups discussing the Willamette Valley.

A small girl was the first to see the Indians. She shrieked. The Indians greatly outnumbered the pioneers and were decked out in war paint. They sat motionless on their ponies. The only sound was the wind moaning through the sage.

In time the chief, wearing a flowing eagle feather headdress, moved ahead of his warriors and came to the edge of the circle of wagons. A frail widow stepped forward with a plate of hot doughnuts. She held it toward the chief.

He eyed it distrustfully, guffawed. Thinking quickly the woman began distributing doughnuts among members of her party. They ate with exaggerated relish, rubbing stomachs and smacking lips to make their pleasure most apparent.

Again the widow approached the chief but still he refused. She offered doughnuts to the warriors. One young brave had the nerve to grab one, took a taste and bolted it in two tremendous bites. The few remaining doughnuts were quickly consumed. The Indians dismounted and came into camp while the women began frying vast quantities of doughnuts.

With the feast in progress, all thought of war between the parties was forgotten. When it was over the Indians rode away. The Ohio train continued on to the Willamette Valley.

THE WORST MEMORY

Eva Brown wrote how her father came west from Wisconsin in the 1800s and that her mother, brother and she joined him later.

She stated: "We traveled by train to the end of the road, which was Rosebud, Montana. From there we went by wagon. I was only a girl at the time but drove one of the teams.

"There were many times on the way to Oregon I had to walk and lead the animals. I thought I had a reasonably heavy pair of shoes but they did not hold up; over the desert the cactus stuck through the soles and in the mountains I had to walk barefoot through snow. The soles were completely gone.

"When we got to where we were going we found Dad had built a frame house, although lumber was hard to come by. Our beds were boards nailed together and mattresses were straw ticks. We brought currant shrubs and potatoes with us from Wisconsin. Father planted them and they did very well.

"Father and Mother filed on a preemption claim and so did my brother and I. All the family lived there together, where the claims joined, in the middle of the wilderness.

"I remember the rattlesnakes. Oh, Lordy, do I remember the rattlesnakes! The worst moment of my life was the time in the dark I reached down to pick an old setting hen from her nest and found a rattler all coiled up there. Oh, that was terrible!"

WOMEN OF THE TRAIL

The women of the Oregon Trail are often perceived in one of two ways: as a hardy, rawboned woman who walked beside the wagon cradling a nursing baby in one arm and firing a rifle at savage Indians with the other; or a pale Eastern-bred woman who had fallen in love with a wandering man and would follow him anywhere.

But the women who came West were more than stereotypes. They cried over the loss of loved ones and sometimes moaned under the hardships of the trail. One woman, who gave birth along the way, looked back on the crossing as an "adventure". Another wrote it was, "the high point of my life".

When they arrived in Oregon the women were just as busy as on the trail. While men cleared fields and planted crops the women cooked, washed, and made homes in the wilderness.

One woman wrote in her diary: "My husband would have turned back a hundred times on the trail and a hundred times since we landed but I won't let him."

Another myth is that pioneer women were in constant danger from Indians. The fact was that women often traded with the Indians, exchanging fresh homemade bread for wild meat, milk and doughnuts for salmon. Only during times of war were Indians a threat.

In time the Indians were gathered onto reservations, the country became more civilized. One pioneer women looked back on the early years and claimed, "Never was there a day I wished myself back East to live."

GAMES

The children of the Oregon Trail had to leave most of their toys behind, but there was no lack of imagination when it came to finding new playthings along the way.

One favorite game of young boys on the wagon train in 1843 was played with the swollen paunch of a slaughtered ox.

Jesse Applegate, who was seven years old, described how the game was played. "The sport consisted in running and butting the head against the paunch and being bounced back, the recoil being in proportion to the force of contact."

It became a favorite game as youngsters showed their courage by running and jumping harder and harder. There was not a particular name for the game until a boy named Andy, with cries of, "Give her goss, Andy," ringing in his ears, jumped at the paunch harder than anyone had dared.

Jesse Applegate told what happened. "Andy backed off much farther than anyone had before, and then charged the paunch at the top of his speed, and when within a couple of yards of the target, leaped up from the ground and came down like a pile driver against the paunch, but he did not bound back. The stomach had closed so tightly around his neck that he could not withdraw his head. We took hold of his legs and pulled him out, but the joke was on Andy and 'Give her goss, Andy' was a favorite game among the boys long after."

FINDING A HORSE

William Savage was a young man walking to Oregon in the company of a wagon train. Every step he wished he had a horse.

Near the crossing of the Sweetwater River he spotted a mount, saddled and tied to a tree some distance off the trail. William called to Captain Umphlette and said he was going to retrieve the horse.

"It's an Indian trick. I've seen 'em use it before to lure a man away from the train. I can't let you go, William," the captain stated.

"I respect your decision," William told him. But after thinking for a moment he suggested, "We should not leave the trap baited and have someone from a following train killed. I better shoot the horse."

He took a prone position for the long shot, but instead of killing the horse the bullet kicked up dirt under its belly. The frightened horse pulled loose, began running in a big circle that brought him near the wagon train. William jumped to his feet, ran forward, grabbed the lead rope and took control of the horse.

The wagon train continued, and riding in the front of the column was William Savage. He was the envy of the others as he rode the horse all the way to Oregon.

William settled in the Willamette Valley, became a stockman and later a banker in Dallas. The horse that carried him to Oregon was turned out to pasture and eventually died of old age.

STARTING OUT

Bill Patton was a young Missourian who fell in love with a girl named Annie Dickens. When Annie's parents decided to emigrate to Oregon, young Bill lost no time signing on as an oxen driver on the same wagon train.

Along the way Bill courted Annie. And then one night with the stars out and the coyotes howling, he asked her to marry him when they reached Oregon.

Somewhere along the way, the money Bill had managed to save was stolen. He couldn't get married until he was financially secure so when they reached the Willamette Valley he went to work splitting rails for 37½ cents per hundred. After he had earned $2.25 he made the necessary arrangements to marry Annie.

The day after the ceremony Bill went back to splitting rails. One day his father-in-law talked to him about the merits of owning land. He also said he would like to have his daughter close by and told Bill the land adjacent to his donation land claim was open for claiming.

When Bill went to file on the land he discovered a fellow by the name of Center had just filed on it. Bill looked up Center. Center listened to the boy, thought about it for a moment and concluded land was available everywhere. Each acre was just as good as the next as far as he was concerned. "All right, lad. I'll sell," he told Bill. "The price for my 160 acres will be one plug of tobacco."

The deal was struck. In the following years Bill and Annie raised nine Patton children on the "home place".

SIGN OF DISTRESS

Early pioneer J.C. Moreland recalled coming to Oregon. He began: "I was born on June 10, 1844, in Tennessee, the youngest of nine. My parents were poor. Most of the neighbors were slave owners. But being unwilling to own slaves and being unable to compete with slave labor, my father decided to move to a free state.

"In the early spring of 1852, we started for Oregon. There were about 40 wagons in our train, and we had 70 men who were able to bear arms. Our company held together until we reached Eastern Oregon, the Grande Ronde Valley, where we broke up and everyone was left to shift for themselves. I remember very distinctly climbing zig-zag in the mountains. Our oxen were so weak we had to throw out everything we could possibly do without.

"The one scene stands out particularly strongly in my mind was when it got as bad as it was going to get. We had eaten the last of our hardtack and the last of our bacon. We were without provisions of any kind. I was sitting on a log near the wagon. Mother was on the wagon tongue. A cold, drizzling rain was falling. We were discouraged.

"I heard a noise from the west and with a boy's curiosity I went down the trail to see what it was. I came running back and excitedly told the others, 'Here comes a man on a fat horse and a fat yoke of oxen pulling his wagon.'

"When he drove up, Father spoke to him and made a sign with his hands I did not understand. The man promptly took several loaves of light bread as well as some boiled beef, cold boiled potatoes and raw onions from his wagon and gave them to Mother. I never remember eating a better meal in my life. I can still taste the delicious onions.

"Afterward I asked my father what made the man give us the food since I knew we had no money to pay for it. Father said, 'My boy, I gave him the sign of distress of a Master Mason.'

"Right then and there I decided to become a Mason."

FLAMING RED HAIR

John Kelley was captain of a wagon train to Oregon. In his later years one of his favorite stories was about an incident that occurred the first week out on the Oregon Trail.

"There was a woman driving a team and wagon," he told, "and for company she had brought along her niece. We were only a hundred miles from Missouri when the woman died. No reason for it. She just died. The niece was left completely alone.

"The girl was young, horribly scatter-brained, and rather homely, too. None of the single men would have anything to do with her. Her only attribute seemed to be the beautiful head of bright red hair that she possessed. It hung in tight curls over her shoulders and down to the middle of her back.

"We crossed into Indian country with the girl driving her aunt's team. One day an Indian hunting party appeared. They showed no signs of hostility and I allowed them to ride alongside and keep us company.

"There was one Indian, mounted on a magnificent black horse, who dropped back and rode beside the red-haired girl. He stared at her but never uttered a word.

"Did he see her as a beautiful goddess? I do not know. But the men, the same ones who had shunned her, now made objections. They told the lovesick brave they did not want him courting one of their women and expelled him from the wagon train. The girl watched her admirer ride over the ridge and commented to one of the women that all she wanted was a man who would worship her.

"That evening the Indian reappeared at the edge of camp. He and his horse stood still as a granite statue. A long moment passed and then the girl went running to him. The Indian reached for her and swung her up behind him. The coal black horse whirled and galloped away.

"At the top of the rise the girl turned back toward the circle of wagons. She waved. And that was the last anyone saw of the girl with the flaming red hair."

WHITE FEATHER

In his reminiscences James Neall related an experience he had on the Oregon Trail in 1848. His party was coming through buffalo country along Platte River when James noticed "... a large Buffaloe bull coming down on the opposite side of the river making for a low range of hills some half mile distant on our side of the river. As I had never killed a buffaloe entirely by myself, I was seized with the idea of killing him in order to say I had killed a buffaloe.

"With this in view, I took an English smooth bore flint-lock musket instead of my rifle of small bore on account of its carrying a larger ball to execute my fell purpose. Having taken note of the direction the bull was taking toward some hills, I laid my course so as to intercept him and proceeded about three-quarters of a mile, and as I raised up on the top of one of the ridges, there was Mr. Bull about twenty yards off, broadside on. I raised my musket and pulled the trigger, and down came the hammer with a crash, but as the wind was blowing fresh right in my teeth, missed fire.

"The sound made Mr. Bull aware of my presence. The shaggy monster stopped and glared at me. Instantly a thousand recollections of tales of a wounded bull in pursuit of a bad marksman flashed thro me, and glancing behind me over a stretch of three-quarters of a mile between me and camp, I doubted my speed, and looking Mr. Bull in the face, I apologized and said, 'It's all a mistake, I intended no insult. You go your way and I'll go mine,' and he did....I confess to showing the 'white feather'."

THE FINAL INSULT

In the spring of 1850 a group of pioneers abandoned homes near Milwaukee, Wisconsin, formed a wagon train and started for Oregon. They encountered stampeding buffalo herds, endured heat, dust, lack of water and rationed food. They saw no Indians — until they reached Snake River.

John James, a small boy at the time, later wrote, "We set camp at Soda Springs, a very cozy-looking place, within sight of Fort Hall. Us youngsters went for a refreshing swim in Snake River and there was a lot of fine grass for the stock.

"We had such a comfortable camp it was thought safe. A guard was not posted that night and in the morning we awakened to find the stock scattered, a number missing; we could only guess they had been run off by Indians.

"A search party was organized and started in pursuit. Downriver, near the crossing, they came across the body of one of our largest oxen, Old Dave. He had been a very independent kind of an ox and I suppose he objected to being captured and tried to turn back. They had cut his throat.

"We only lost the one ox, but Mr. Robert Foster, traveling with one wagon, lost his entire team. There stood the wagon, wife and children, helpless in the wilds, a lonely-looking prospect staring them in the face. Our people contributed each what they could spare and re-outfitted Mr. Foster with a make-shift team.

"The thing that really got our goats was the way the Indians acted. They stayed in plain sight, on the opposite side of the river, just beyond rifle range, and tried all sorts of antics to provoke us to shoot. We could not even accept the challenge of the savages as they taunted us by stooping over and offering their backsides for targets."

FIRE SPIRIT

The Indian guide lay on his belly, ear to the ground. When he finally rose he wore a very serious look. One of the group of white men being led over the Oregon Trail mocked the guide, "Make heap big medicine, huh, Red Thunder?"

Before swinging onto the back of his pony Red Thunder somberly stated, "Fire Spirit live in cloud. Afraid Fire Spirit him come awake." The men guffawed. There was not the slightest trace of smoke carried on the south wind, no sign of fire on the broad green plains. They laughed at their strange Indian guide, told him to lead on.

At midday they pulled up for dinner. While the white men dined, the Indian walked a short distance from camp and again put his ear to the ground. Quickly he leaped to his feet, searched the horizon until spotting a smudge of smoke far to the south. Fire was running before the wind. The wind was blowing strong.

Red Thunder made toward camp crying, "Fire Spirit awake!" He jumped on his horse and led the others on a dead run toward the safety of a distant, bald knob. During the wild race the wind carried the acrid smell of smoke, the horses snorted and ran all the faster. Live embers were in the air. Spotfires were starting everywhere. Wild animals were fleeing. The heavens were black and suffocating smoke blocked the path.

Red Thunder led the white men to the knob and the men dug heels into their mounts' shoulders. The horses struggled uphill where the earth was bare and the fire could not burn. Around them, on all sides, a living sea of fire surged and then swept past.

Again glorious sunshine returned to blue sky and fleecy white clouds overhead made the landscape of the prairie all the more black.

MISSOURI MULE

William Jenkins was a boy of ten when his family headed west over the Oregon Trail. In his later years, living on the southern Oregon coast, William would sometimes tell the wagon train story of his standing guard one night.

"Well, there we were," he would say, drawing out the words, "camped in the middle of nowhere. I had been pestering the men for weeks to let me stand guard and that night they let me. Figured we were out of Indian country, I'd guess.

"They gave me explicit instructions — said if anything of a suspicious nature, anything at all, happened during the night I was to signal by firing a shot in the air. One of them gave me an old blunderbuss. They all went to bed, to sleep. I could hear some snoring. A sliver of moon was casting an eerie light, not enough to see anything but dim shadows. There were night sounds. A coyote howled and one of the dogs from the wagon train barked. A horse nickered and pawed the ground.

"Like I said, you couldn't see much of anything, but there was this Missouri mule in close near me and the fire. All at once that mule's ears shot forward, pointing into the dark like something was out there. I figured that was enough, cranked off a round and the camp was instantly in turmoil, men dressed in longjohns, armed to the teeth, running around looking for someone to shoot.

"I explained why I blazed away. They scolded me, said, 'The darn kid woke us up for nothing.' But next morning they found an Indian hair rope down among the horses; some Indian had evidently been fixing to steal the horses. I told them, I says, 'See, that old Missouri mule wasn't so dumb after all.' "

BAD FEELINGS

In the spring of 1847 one of the largest wagon trains to come west started from the Missouri River. It consisted of more than one thousand wagons and five thousand people separated into thirty divisions. When all the wagons were underway, with spacing between the divisions, the train stretched a distance of one hundred miles.

Included among the travelers were farmers, merchants, clergymen, doctors, college professors, lawyers and a future governor. Along the way lovers' vows were exchanged and vows were broken. Babies were born. People died and were often buried in the middle of the Oregon Trail so their graves could not be detected by the Indians.

The divisions bringing up the rear endured the most trying conditions. Those who went before them had not maintained sanitary campgrounds. Their stock — ten thousand head of cattle, one thousand horses and several hundred mules and sheep — had cut a swath miles wide on either side of the trail, leaving very little grass. Lack of wild game was another problem.

Most troubling of all were the Indians. They resented the large number of whites moving through their country and took it out on the rear divisions, harassing and pilfering at every opportunity.

After reaching The Dalles, the last divisions waited to arrange passage downriver or to begin the climb over the Cascades on Barlow's Trail. It was here, at the end of the Oregon Trail, that the bad feelings between the whites and the Indians erupted. In the short battle an Indian killed an emigrant. In retaliation several Indians, including a chief, were killed.

HIDDEN STRENGTH

A wagon train of Missouri pioneers was struggling through the Columbia Gorge. The wagons and everyone on the train were loaded on ferries except for six men who drove the stock overland.

One of the ferries was manned by an inexperienced crew. As they came toward the landing above a series of falls the current caught them and spun their raft headlong toward the dull roar and the rising mist of the cataracts.

The six men who had gone with the stock were waiting at the landing and heard the cries for help. A deck hand on board the stricken raft had presence of mind enough to throw a rope toward shore.

It uncoiled, and fell short. The six men ran forward into the water but could not reach the end of the rope. Quickly they formed a human chain and the last man grabbed the end of the rope. Using every ounce of strength the six were slowly able to gain control of the raft. It began a gentle arc toward shore.

42

PURE JOY

The sun played with mirages, shimmered the sage and scattered juniper. The heat and desolation added to the misery of the Barkhart family. They were thirsty and hungry. With no meat for two weeks and no flour for one, they were on rations of three swigs of water a day.

The loose stock smelled the Snake River first and stampeded. The oxen pulling the wagon broke into a trot and family members struggled barefoot to keep up. One by one they stumbled into the river.

They satisfied their thirst. The sun began to set and the clouds on the horizon took on colors of gold and red. They were facing a long, hungry night. The Barkhart family came together, dropped to their knees and prayed to God for something to eat.

"Antelope! I see antelope!" cried one of the boys, pointing to a distant ridge top. C.D. Barkhart grabbed his rifle, lay on the ground and took aim. What seemed like an eternity passed before the sudden wash of the concussion and the booming crash of the rifle sounded. One antelope fell dead. A loaded rifle was handed to C.D. and he fired again. A second animal went down and a whoop of joy went up.

43

PLAYING INDIAN

Annie was one of seven children in the Griffin family. In the spring of 1880 the Griffins started west from South Dakota in a wagon pulled by oxen. They were accompanied by four other wagons.

Across the Plains they fought mud and strong winds. Climbing over the Rocky Mountains they battled snow. Progress was slow. In Idaho the emigrants laid over for a few weeks to rest the stock. During that time Mrs. Griffin gave birth to another child and her oldest daughter fell in love with a young man in the train and became engaged.

The four families had children about the same ages and they spent the layover playing games. The favorite was Indian and they took turns attacking the wagons, throwing sticks as make-believe arrows.

After three weeks the wagon train continued and eventually reached southern Oregon. One morning after breakfast the children were playing games as the adults broke camp. Annie was an Indian. She came running off the side hill, whooping as savagely as she could. One of her sisters was playing an emigrant and to escape crawled up into the wagon box. Annie went after her.

An older brother had laid one of his pistols on the bed in the wagon. The sister grabbed it and when Annie appeared the little girl pointed the pistol at her and pulled the trigger. There was a flash of fire and a tremendous boom.

The slug missed Annie and embedded itself in the wagon behind, missing Mrs. Griffin, who was visiting the neighbor, by only a few inches. Never again were the children allowed to play Indian.

SHEEPMAN

At the age of 26 David Stump, a surveyor and teacher, gave up on life in Iowa and sought a new beginning in Oregon. But David had no wagon, no money and was only able to convince a captain of a wagon train to take him along after giving an exhibition of his skill as a marksman. He walked all the way to Oregon and paid his way by supplying wild game to the pioneers.

The wagon train arrived in the Willamette Valley in the fall of 1846. Two years later gold was discovered at Sutter's Mill and David was lured to the California gold fields. He spent a year at the diggings and in that time managed to accumulate a sizable fortune. Then he journeyed east and purchased a large flock of sheep which he and several herders started over the Oregon Trail. It was one of the first flocks of sheep ever brought West.

At Snake River David arranged for a group of Indians to use their canoes to help swim the sheep to the opposite side. For their help David promised them all the sheep that drowned in the process.

They started the crossing early in the morning and it progressed smoothly with more and more sheep gathered, bleating on the Oregon bank. At first very few sheep were drowned and then all at once sheep were dying left and right. It was discovered, by closely watching the Indians, they were paddling alongside the swimming sheep and stealthily holding their heads under water.

The majority of the flock did make it to shore and David and the herders again started west. They reached the Willamette Valley and David had enough gold remaining in his saddle bags to purchase 2,300 acres of choice grasslands. Thereafter David Stump was known as "Father of the Sheep Industry in Oregon".

46

BUFFALO STAMPEDE

The Oregon-bound wagon train was crossing the Plains. One day nine-year-old George Himes rode his horse ahead to get out of the dust and to scout the way. He was about a mile in front and on the top of a low rise when, in the distance, he thought he could see a low, rolling fog. He watched this strange phenomenon for long minutes before it dawned on him what it was. He dismounted, placed his ear on the ground and heard the distant rumblings of a buffalo stampede.

George galloped his horse back to the wagon train. Even before he was within hearing distance he was shouting, "Buffalo!" at the top of his lungs. He wildly pointed behind, to the now visible dust cloud.

"Circle the wagons!" commanded the captain. The lead wagon came around to meet the last. There was no time to waste as the men unhitched the oxen and brought them and the loose stock inside the wagon corral.

Thousands of hooves struck the ground with a sound like rolling thunder. And then the front wall of the advancing herd could be seen. It appeared they were on a direct line toward the cluster of canvas-topped wagons. At the last possible instant the leaders changed directions and passed to one side.

The herd was like a surging brown river. Occasionally the choking dust would part to reveal an individual cow or bull, foaming at the mouth, breath coming short and fast. It was a terrifying and awesome spectacle.

For more than an hour the herd passed. As the dust slowly began to settle the pioneers discovered the buffalo had continued on for a quarter mile, down a gradual hill to a cut-bank above the Platte River. Now only a few buffalo remained alive, roaming around, bellowing. The others, thousands upon thousands, had gone over the embankment.

FRIENDS

A kid by the name of Sitton wanted to come west and managed to join a wagon train for Oregon. He was likeable enough and got along with everyone until he had a run-in with the captain.

Sitton was standing night guard, he was tired and his eyesight and judgment were not the best. He thought he saw an Indian and fired his rifle. A company of men armed with rifles and lanterns went to have a look and discovered the kid had killed the captain's favorite mule. The captain banished Sitton from the train, told him to pack what he could carry and start east, they way they had come. Sitton had no choice, he made a pack.

Several weeks behind was a second wagon train and in this company was a fellow about Sitton's age. His name was Charley Fendall. One day he was hunting in front of the train when he spotted someone afoot, traveling east.

The paths of the two, Sitton and Fendall, had crossed. Sitton told his story and rode double with Fendall back to camp. From that moment the two were inseparable friends. They eventually made it to Oregon and spent the first winter in a cabin on Panther Creek. In spring they stalked out adjoining land claims in the Willamette Valley, married sisters and remained friends for the rest of their days.

THE ARROW

An hour of daylight remained and the evening wind was blowing in the pioneers' faces. The wagon train captain turned in his saddle and made an arcing motion with his free hand, signaling the drivers to circle the wagons.

Tonight the wagon train would be camped at the edge of Indian country and the pioneers were wary. Their worst fears were confirmed when one of the men, Nicholas Lee, discovered a message freshly scratched into the sunbleached skull of a buffalo. It stated, "Indians hostile."

The captain called a meeting, instructed the pioneers to extinguish cook fires as soon as possible after dinner. He doubled the usual number of guards.

Night descended and at one of the camp fires a young motherless girl was hurrying to finish mending her brother's trousers. She suddenly screamed and fell over. An arrow was embedded in her thigh.

A number of heavy blankets were thrown over the bows of a covered wagon. In the dim light of a lantern emergency surgery was performed, the arrow removed. Examination disclosed the leg bone was broken and the leg was set in a temporary splint with two ramrods. In the morning the wound was treated, the leg set properly and the wagon train went on its way.

THANK THE OX

John Southerlin took the first watch. The wagons were circled and the campfires smoking. The oxen were grazing along the bank of the Snake River. To the west the sun had begun to slip from the sky leaving behind a puddle of bright yellow and orange.

Perhaps it was the quick alarm of a rattlesnake or maybe only the wind through the sage that startled the oxen. They suddenly, and for no apparent reason, stampeded into the river. The current was strong, swift and deceptive. In a very short time the oxen were swept into the main stream.

John, a large athletic man, never hesitated. He kicked off his boots and dove into the swirling water. He swam, trying to make a big circle around the oxen. He succeeded in positioning himself between the swimming oxen and the opposite shore. He yelled at them, splashed the water with his hands. The oxen turned.

By then John was beginning to flounder. He did not have enough remaining strength to pull himself free of the clutches of the Snake.

A voice boomed out across the water. It was Porter Wilson, one of the other emigrants who saw what was happening and had chased along the bank to keep up with the action. He hollered, "Grab that ox by the tail."

There was one ox near John and with a mighty effort he swam to it and grabbed hold of its tail. The ox pulled him to shore.

Later, John graciously thanked Porter for saving his life. But Porter told him, "Don't thank me. I never got wet. Thank the ox."

JUSTICE SERVED

Caleb Greenwood and his three sons met a wagon train in 1845 at Fort Hall on the Snake River and tried to persuade the pioneers to abandon their Oregon dream and follow them back to California.

The next morning eight wagons broke away and followed the Greenwoods. After three days of traveling south Caleb left his three sons in charge of guiding the wagons while he returned to Fort Hall to persuade more emigrants to follow.

The oldest of the boys, John, was in command. One day, coming across a flat dotted by sagebrush and cut by gullies, an Indian jumped from behind a sagebrush and scared his horse. The horse reared and John nearly fell off. Several men in the party laughed and that made John angry.

"I'll kill 'im!" he declared and pulled his rifle from the scabbard. The Indian threw up his hands.

"He didn't mean no harm. Don't shoot 'im," the men remonstrated. And when it looked as though John would defy them and shoot, they called out to the Indian, "Run for your life!" John followed him with the rifle, fired and the Indian went down.

That evening Caleb Greenwood rode into camp. He called the pioneers together, said he had come across the Indian still alive and had put him out of his misery. Then he called, "The man who shot him through the back is a murderer."

When informed the murderer was his own son John, he grew very serious. For a moment Caleb stood with head bowed and then he straightened and announced, "He must die. I give orders to shoot John on sight as you would any wild animal."

John, who had positioned himself at the outer perimeter of camp, jumped on his horse and escaped. But justice was served. Not long after, he was involved in a fight over a game of cards and was stabbed to death.

REMEMBERING

Benjamin Bonney was a seven-year-old boy when he came over the Oregon Trail. His most vivid memories of the ordeal were when they departed Independence, Missouri, the last settlement, and the nights they were trapped on the Plains in thunderstorms.

"When we passed through Independence," he recalled some years later, "back in 1845, it was the last trading point on the frontier. The Indians were camped all around and were anxious to trade buffalo robes for shirts, powder, lead or firewater. Preferably the latter. Father bought four finely tanned buffalo robes from the Indians. There were several stores at Independence and a number of blacksmith shops and wagon shops, as well as livery stables and hotels.

"The things I remember scaring me the most were the thunderstorms that took place at night on the Plains. The thunder was incessant, and the lightning was so brilliant it lit up the country all around. The men chained the oxen so they could not stampede. They would bellow and bawl. Sometimes our tents would be blown down and the covers blown off the wagons. Then the rain would come and we would be like drowning rats.

"Unless you have been through it you have no idea of the confusion resulting from a storm on the Plains. Oxen bellowing, children crying, men shouting and the thunder rolling like a constant salvo of artillery. One second bright as day, and the next black as the depths of the pit."

SLEEPLESS NIGHT

The Pringle family came across the Oregon Trail in 1846, but veered away from the main route to take an alternate trail to the Willamette Valley over the high desert.

It was late in the fall before they reached the Umpqua Valley. They were facing snow and starvation. Only one horse was still alive, a broken-down mare. It was decided the oldest boy, 14-year-old Octavius, must ride her to the Willamette Valley and bring back supplies.

The first two days Octavius rode in company of two mountain men; the third day he reached the Willamette Valley. He purchased dried peas and wheat graham flour, all he thought the poor mare could carry, and led her back toward his starving family.

It was mid-afternoon, a gloomy, rainy day somewhere in the mountains, when Octavius came upon a bear track—an unusually large bear track. It was fresh; muddy water still filtered into it. For five miles he tagged along behind the bear. Just before dark it wandered off the trail. That night the boy ate a mixture of graham flour and water from a tin cup and spread his blanket beneath an old fir tree.

At midnight Octavius was awakened by crashing in the brush. He felt heavy breathing on the nape of his neck and, faster than greased lightning, he shinnied up the fir tree. All night he perched on the limb. It was cold and wet. Below him he occasionally heard branches crack and break. He sat tight, knowing it was the bear.

At first light he discovered the cause of his fright — an old, emaciated emigrant cow left behind to die. He drove the bag of bones away and with utmost disgust hit the trail. Two days later he found the wagon and a feast of boiled peas and graham bread was prepared.

They reached the Willamette Valley just as the early winter floods began, stumbling into the clearing beside the cabin of Eugene Skinner, founder of Eugene.

TOUGH

Talk about tough. Elizabeth Geer had it tough.

The Geer family came to Oregon by wagon, landing in Portland late in 1848. Elizabeth's husband was on his last leg, confined to bed. With seven children in tow it fell on Elizabeth to find a place where they could pass the winter.

She sold the wagon for enough to pay the rent on a lean-to off a cabin, hired two men to carry her husband to their new quarters and she and the children packed the bed and their few meager belongings.

Elizabeth prayed every night that her husband would get well and that conditions would become easier. But the prayers were not answered. Things became worse. Food was scarce and expensive: pork ran ten cents a pound and potatoes were seventy-five cents per bushel. But the Indians sold salmon for four cents a pound and the family subsisted on an almost exclusive diet of fish.

It rained and rained. The roof, instead of shedding water, trapped it. The worst leak was where the fireplace came through the roof. The fireplace was like a dam and when it rained hard, water tumbled over the rock like a series of miniature waterfalls. Then the fire would hiss. And if it rained long enough the coals would drown. One time Elizabeth dipped six pails of water from the hearth.

Most disturbing of all was that in addition to a sick husband Elizabeth had to watch her children fall ill. Five were down, too sick to move, at one time. Elizabeth made them as comfortable as she could.

On the first day of February, Elizabeth wrote in her diary: "This day my dear husband, my last remaining friend, died." The following day she entered: "Today we buried my earthly companion. Now I know what none but widows know; that is, how comfortless is a widow's life; especially when left in a strange land without money or friends, and the care of seven children."

THAT WINTER!

It took the Ross family six months in a covered wagon to reach Oregon. They spent the first winter, 1860-61, in a log cabin in the small settlement of Portland, but come spring Mr. Ross claimed homestead land bordering the Columbia River.

The next spring the Ross farm flooded. Mr. Ross became discouraged and moved his family downriver, to a section of high ground surrounded by the Clatskanie Slough. Years later Chas. Ross, who had been a small boy at the time, recalled, "We were isolated, seven miles to the closest neighbors and no wagon road, no trail, it was all by rowboat.

"The first winter we spent there it got terrible bad cold, early on, and Father went out and brought back a supply of flour. The river froze behind him. Then on top of the cold it started to snow. It would thaw a little during the day and snow and freeze at night. We children would walk along on top — snow built up to four feet deep — and sometimes it was stiff enough to support Father. For fear of running out of matches we kept a fire going all the time.

"But, oh, the desolation! The worst part was we started the winter with fifty head of cattle and only three ton of wild marsh hay. Father had figured the steers would be able to range for themselves while the hay was intended for the cows that would be calving. The hay was soon gone and Father resorted to chopping down maple trees so the cattle could eat the twigs. When a tree would fall, how the cattle would flounder through the snow for it.

"The cattle soon began to die. They would lie in their tracks and freeze; the meat was in perfect shape for weeks. The cold snap lasted three months. We lost half the cattle.

"After such a winter the folks were disheartened at what we had been forced to endure and were determined not to pass another such winter. We packed up, moved to the settlement of Portland."

THE BOY AND THE SHADOW

After the Civil War the Krewson family decided to leave the troubled times behind and move west to Oregon. Several neighboring families joined in and they formed a small wagon company.

On the Plains they came across a grisly scene, the wagon train ahead had been attacked by Indians. Men, women and children had been massacred and it was so fresh the wagon remains were still smoldering. They stopped long enough to bury the dead and then went on.

They reached Snake River, crossed over and started up Burnt river canyon and into the Blue Mountains. Here they killed a number of deer and a feast was held.

One of the Krewson boys, who was barely fourteen years old, had been begging to take a turn as night guard. Since they had not seen any Indians for a number of days the boy was told he would get his wish, that he would take the first guard shift. While the others retired the boy paced back and forth, feeling very grown up and self-important.

Something, a shadow in the moonlight, moved. The boy watched it. A shadow creeping forward, stopping, creeping forward again.

"Halt!" the boy shouted. The shadow moved forward again. Up came the boy's rifle. He sighted down the barrel, pulled the trigger. Fire licked the night.

The camp was thrown into an uproar. Men, armed to the teeth, some with lanterns, crowded around the Krewson boy and demanded to know what he was shooting at. The boy led them to the dark shadow at the edge of camp. There they found not an Indian but a black bear, apparently attracted by the smell of venison, with a bullet in its head.

THE OLD MAN OF THE TRAIL

Ezra Meeker first came to the Oregon Country in 1852, crossing the Oregon Trail by wagon and oxen team. Fifty-four years later he proposed to retrace the route and mark it with trail markers, preserving it for future generations.

Meeker solicited money in Portland for his trip, but received only $200. The general feeling in the city was no one wanted to contribute to a fund sending a 76-year-old man on a trip which most likely would kill him. But Meeker was determined. He hitched a pair of oxen named Twist and Dave to a wagon and started east.

The small towns in eastern Oregon — Echo, Pendleton, La Grande, Baker — gave Meeker rousing welcomes. The school children went on penny drives, collecting pennies to give to the pioneer who promised to put up trail markers. At Boise a crowd of 3,000 turned out for a parade led by Twist and Dave.

From the end of the trail to the Great Plains, Meeker raised more than one hundred cedar trail markers. His plan was to drive Twist and Dave all the way to Washington, D.C., where he would ask the President for help in establishing more markers. But in Nebraska the faithful Twist died. The journey was interrupted while Meeker hiked to the Omaha stockyards to purchase a five-year-old steer he named Dandy.

On November 29, 1907, with Dave and Dandy dodging the traffic on Pennsylvania Avenue, Meeker drove his wagon onto the front lawn of the White House. President Teddy Roosevelt came out to pose with the outfit and the colorful white-haired pioneer.

Meeker made one more trip over the Oregon Trail before his death in 1928 at the age of 98. He flew the route in an airplane.

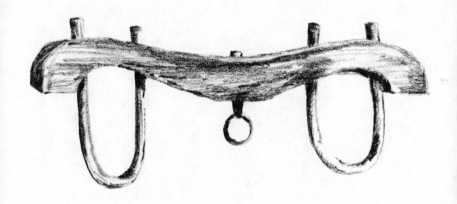